NO BULLSHIT BUSINESS PLAN

HOW TO WRITE A BUSINESS PLAN

EASILY AND CONVINCINGLY

A simple guide to help you write a great business plan even if you have never done so before.

Brought to you by StartUP Crest

Startup Jahswill

This book is part of the business startup guide brought to you by StartUP Crest, a leading business development company with focus on startups and small businesses. You can access more of our resources at startupcrest.com

Contact: info@startupcrest.com

08033867541

DEDICATION

To all the young entrepreneurs and startups working hard every day to make something out of nothing. I feel your struggle because it's a path I have been walking.

◆ ◆ ◆

ACKNOWLEDGEMENT

Let me first of all acknowledge the CEO of Karone Group, Nelson Eduzobe, who together we started Karone Photo World Ltd in 2011. It gave me a bigger platform to work with and pushed me to where I am today.

Secondly, Chinwe (aka Rendy) for reading through the initial draft and making very important inputs that has led to this final piece.

Also, there are my bankers and friends in the banking industry who answered my numerous questions while researching this book. Thank you guys, your patience and insight made this book valuable.

Most importantly though, is my wife Given and my daughter Kemzi, who both were patient with me throughout the period of writing. There were days I didn't have time for them but they still loved me notwithstanding. My beautiful wife especially, for believing in me always and supporting me through the good and bad times, I love you both girls.

INTRODUCTION

Back in 2011, I had started a small business with my brother. It was one of the most exciting times of my life! I have always wanted to build a business empire that can impact lives and pay the bills. Those were my "career day" wishes in junior school.

This was not my first attempt at business though. There have been Piick Me Ads, SwiftTech Integrated Solutions and a few others. All had failed because of lack of funds to market and grow the business. So, this was another opportunity to try again. This time, with a "financial backer". Heck, my brother was working in a multinational oil company.

However, it soon dawned on me that our business is not my brother's personal property. Thus, I have to find other means of raising capital. That was when the task of writing a real business plan first hit me in the face.

Every financial institution I approached, be it a bank or lending houses, all wanted to see a business plan. Sure, I had written business plans before, but not when the life of my business depended on it.

So, I quickly sat down to write my first real business plan. I researched every article that is worth its salt online. Bought business books written by famous authors like Brian Tracy, Robert Kiyosaki and many others. When I was done, researching and writing, I sent my business loan proposal to my bank.

The Response...

The response I got was both disappointing and interesting. "Hi Mr Jahswill, you have a great business plan, but we are not able to finance you at this time as there are embargo on how much we can loan out per quarter, and we have hit that limit".

I was devastated but encouraged. Encouraged because they replied. And that they found my business plan to be GREAT! I immediately opened a business bank account with another bank, waited for a few months and sent in the exact same request. This time, we got financed!

And this bank has consistently financed us for four years straight. The secret was a GREAT business plan. It spoke to my bank account manager, my bank branch manager and the risk assessment guys at my bank.

Since then, I have written several GREAT business plans that have been financed by financial institutions and investors. In 2018, my business plan was among those selected for funding by the YOU-WIN Connect program in Nigeria. In fact, my pitch presentation was so moving that the facilitators asked for my contact at the end of the 3-day Master Class organized for participants!

I know you want that kind of success too. Its why I wrote this book to help startups and small business owners like you.

It is possible, and I will help you do that.

This book has been written to guide you to doing just that. Not just get a bank loan, but write a business plan for any audience. Whether that is a bank, a group of investors, or a grant awarding panel.

This book will help you write a GREAT business plan that you will be proud of and investors and financial institutions will love. But before we begin, let us quickly define what a business plan is and see some basic things to keep in mind before you begin writing your business plan.

Table of Contents

DEDICATION

ACKNOWLEDGEMENT

Introduction

Part One: Setting the Stage for a Successful Business Plan

Chapter One

Business Plan Basics

Part Two: The Business Plan

Chapter Two

Executive summary

Chapter Three

The Opportunity

Chapter Four

Execution

Chapter Five

Company Overview and Team

Chapter Six

Financial plan

Chapter Seven

Appendix

Part Three: Additional Guidelines

Chapter Eight

Common Business Plan Mistakes and How to Avoid Them

About the author

Entrepreneur | Public Speaker | Business Coach

PART ONE: SETTING THE STAGE FOR A SUCCESSFUL BUSINESS PLAN

This section will help you set the path for writing your business plan successfully. It covers the definition of a business plan, basic rules to keep in mind while writing, and reasons why you need a business plan.
Dive in now!

CHAPTER ONE
Business Plan Basics

What is a Business Plan?

A business plan is a written document that clearly describes how a business will strategically attain its goals. It highlights the nature of the business, its sales and marketing strategy, business background, financial expectations and systems.

A business plan is like the blueprint for a house. It has the floor plan and the structural drawings that show what goes where.

◆ ◆ ◆

Here are three basic rules to keep in mind when writing your business plan.

1. Keep it short

Business plans should be short and concise.

There are two reasons for this.

First, you want your business plan to be read (and no one is going to read a 100-page or even 40-page business plan).

Second, your business plan should be a tool you use to run and grow your business, something you continue to use and refine over time. You should be able to take a quick glance from time to time to check your progress. It's also wise to leave room for adjustment of ideas.

An excessively long business plan is a huge hassle to revise—you're almost guaranteed that your plan will be relegated to a desk drawer, never to be seen again.

2. Know your audience - use simple, easy to understand language.

Write your plan using language that your audience will understand.

For example, if your company is developing a complex scientific process, but your prospective investors aren't scientists, avoid jargon, or acronyms that won't be familiar.

Instead of this:

"Our patent-pending technology is a stand-alone multi-solution to new and existing Immunodeficiency-related diseases. When used with acetaminophen, our product provides relief and non-residual CaRTF cell growth."

Write this:

"Our patent-pending product is a one-stop solution to people with low immune system and help to relieve related diseases. When used with paracetamol, our product provides relief and leaves no traces of the drug in the body".

You get the idea, right?

Accommodate your readers, and keep explanations of your product simple and direct, using terms that everyone can understand. You can always use the appendix of your plan to provide the full specs if needed.

Pro Tip:

If you must use technical terms to state certain things, be sure to explain them immediately. Also, remember to add a glossary of

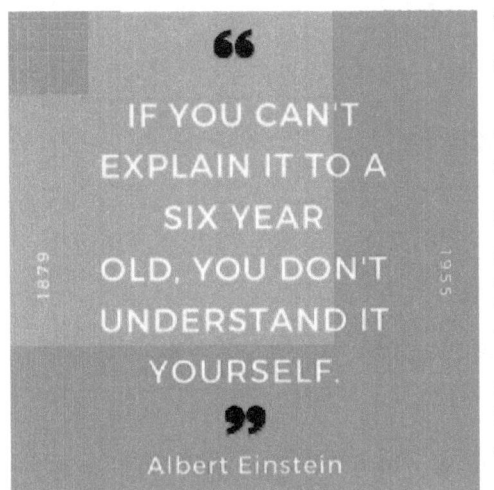

66

IF YOU CAN'T
EXPLAIN IT TO A
SIX YEAR
OLD, YOU DON'T
UNDERSTAND IT
YOURSELF.

99

Albert Einstein

terms in the appendix section of your business plan.

3. Don't be intimidated

The vast majority of business owners and entrepreneurs aren't business experts. Just like you, they're learning as they go and don't have degrees in business. So, do not be intimidated by the thoughts of writing a business plan!

Writing a business plan may seem like a big hurdle, but it doesn't have to be. You know your business—you're the expert on it. For that reason alone, writing a business plan and then leveraging your plan for growth won't be nearly as challenging as you think.

And you don't have to start with the full, detailed business plan that I'm going to describe here. In fact, it can be much easier to start with a simple, one-page business plan—what we call a Lean Plan—and then come back and build a slightly longer, more detailed business plan later.

Note:

Even when applying for grants, investments and loans; most times you are required to first submit a few details about your business. A Lean Plan such as the Business Model Canvas can help you scale this hurdle very easily.

Why You Need a Business Plan

Remember how we compared a business plan to a building plan earlier? Just like you wouldn't just walk into a piece of land and start laying blocks, you shouldn't just launch a business without having a plan. The plan will show what needs to be done, when it should be done, and how it should be done.

Below are some specific reasons why you need a business plan:

1. Secure funding for your business

2. Attract investors and partners to your business

3. Validate your business idea

4. Determine best metrics for measuring business success

5. Drawing board for your business

6. Sell your business

Now that you've reviewed what a business plan is, and why you need one to start and grow your business, it's time to dig into the process of actually writing a business plan.

This book is a step-by-step guide. In it, I'll take you through every stage of writing a business plan that will actually help you achieve your goals.

If however, you're just looking for a downloadable template to get you started, you can skip ahead and download it now. Or, if you just want to see what a completed business plan looks like, check out our library of free sample business plans.

Let us begin.

PART TWO: THE BUSINESS PLAN

Elements of a Business Plan
Now that we have the rules of writing a business plan out of the way, the rest of this book will explain what should be in your business plan, what you should skip, the critical financial projections, and links to additional resources that can help jump-start your plan.

Right here are the six basic components of the business plan you're going to write.

1. Executive summary

This is a brief overview of the business and the plans you have for it. It shouldn't be more than two pages. Even though it is the first part of your business plan, it is usually best written last. After you have written other sections, this part will be a summary of those other parts.

2. Opportunity

This section answers these questions: What are you actually selling and how are you solving a problem (or "need") for your market? Who is your target market and competition?

3. Execution

How are you going to take your opportunity and turn it into a business? This section will cover your marketing and sales plans, operations, and your milestones and metrics for success.

This is where you will outline your strategy for success.

4. Company and management summary

Investors look for great teams in addition to great ideas. Use this chapter to describe your current team and who you need to hire. You will also provide a quick overview of your legal structure, location, and history if you're already up and running.

5. Financial plan

Your business plan isn't complete without a financial forecast. I'll tell you what to include in your financial plan.

6. Appendix

If you need more space for additional details such as product images, market research questionnaire and results, use the appendix for those details.

Let's get down to the details of each section of your business plan and focus on building one that your investors and lenders will want to read.

CHAPTER TWO
Executive summary

The executive summary of your business plan introduces your company, explains what you do, and lays out what you're looking for from your readers. Structurally, it is the first chapter of your business plan. And while it's the first thing that people will read, I generally advise that you write it last. Why?

Because once you know the details of your business inside and out, you will be better prepared to write your executive summary. After all, this section is a summary of everything else you're going to write about.

Ideally, the executive summary can act as a stand-alone document that covers the highlights of your detailed plan. In fact, it's very common for investors to ask for only the executive summary when they are evaluating your business. If they like what they see in the executive summary, they'll often follow up with a request for a complete plan, a pitch presentation, and more in-depth financials.

Since this document is such a critical component of your business plan, you'll want to make sure that it's as clear and concise as possible. Cover the key highlights of your business, but don't get into too much detail. This part should not take more than one or two pages. It should be designed in a way that will arouse the interest of your investors and spur them to positive actions.

The critical components of a winning executive summary

One sentence business overview

At the top of the page, right under your business name, include a one-sentence overview of your business that sums up the essence of what you are doing.

This can be a tagline, but its often more effective if the sentence describes what your company actually does. This is also known as your value proposition.

For example, Africa's richest man Dangote's company tagline is: Providing basic needs.

Problem

In one or two sentences, summarize the problem you are solving in the market. Every business is solving a problem for its customers and filling a need in the market.

Solution

This is your product or service. How are you addressing the problem you have identified in the market? Is the solution novel, innovative or simply an improved version of an existing solution?

Target market

Who is your target market, or your ideal customer? How many of them are there? It's important here to be specific.

If you're a clothe company, you aren't targeting "everyone" just because everyone needs to put on clothes. You're most likely targeting a specific market segment such as "style-conscious men" or "dinner-goers." This will make it much easier for you to target your marketing and sales efforts and attract the kinds of customers that are most likely to buy from you.

Competition

How is your target market solving their problem today? Are there alternatives or substitutes in the market?

Every business has some form of competition and it's critical to provide an overview in your executive summary. Just a sentence or two will suffice.

Company overview and team

Provide a brief overview of your team and a short explanation of why you and your team are the right people to take your idea to market.

Investors put an enormous amount of weight on the team—even more than on the idea—because even a great idea needs great execution in order to become a reality.

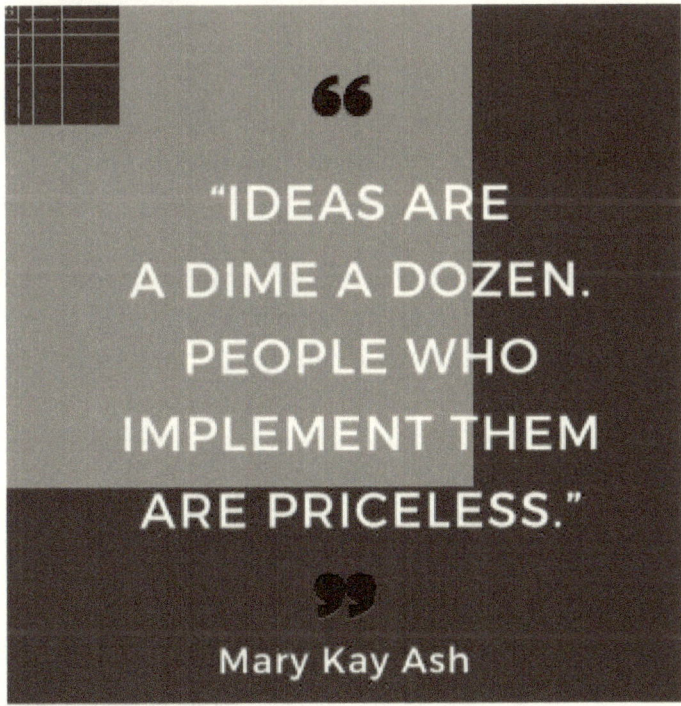

"IDEAS ARE A DIME A DOZEN. PEOPLE WHO IMPLEMENT THEM ARE PRICELESS."

Mary Kay Ash

Financial summary

Highlight the key aspects of your financial plan, ideally with a chart that shows your planned sales, expenses, and profitability.

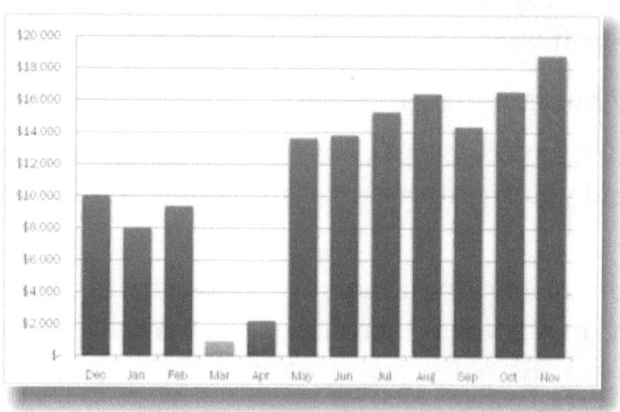

Financial Summary Chart

If your business model (i.e., how you make money) needs additional explanation, this is where you would do it.

Funding requirements

If you are writing a business plan to get a bank loan or because you're asking angel investors or venture capitalists for funding, you must include the details of what you need in the executive summary.

Don't bother to include terms of a potential investment, as that will always be negotiated later. Instead, just include a short statement indicating how much money you need to raise.

Milestones and traction

The last key element of an executive summary that investors will want to see is the progress that you've made so far and future milestones that you intend to hit. If you can show that your potential customers are already interested in - or perhaps already buying your product or service, this is great to highlight.

Pro Tip:

You can skip the executive summary (or greatly reduce it in scope) if you are writing an internal business plan that's purely a strategic guide for your company. In that case, you can do away with details about the management team, funding requirements, and traction, and instead treat the executive summary as an overview of the strategic direction of the company, to ensure that all team members are on the same page.

CHAPTER THREE
The Opportunity

"A problem well stated is a problem half solved."

--John Dewey

There are four main chapters in a business plan - opportunity, execution, company overview, and financial plan. The opportunity chapter of your business plan is where the real meat of your plan lives - it includes information about the problem that you're solving, your solution, who you plan to sell to, and how your product or service fits into the existing competitive landscape.

You'll also use this section of your business plan to demonstrate what sets your solution apart from others, and how you plan to expand your offerings in the future.

People who read your business plan will already know a little bit about your business because they read your executive summary. But this chapter is still hugely important because it's where you expand on your initial overview, providing more details and answering additional questions that you won't cover in the executive summary.

◆ ◆ ◆

The problem and solution

Start the opportunity chapter by describing the problem that you are solving for your customers. What is the primary pain point for them? How are they solving their problems today? Maybe the existing solutions to your customer's problem are very expensive or cumbersome. For a business with a physical location, perhaps there aren't any existing solutions within reasonable driving distance.

Defining the problem you are solving for your customers is by far the most critical element of your business plan and crucial for your business success. If you can't identify a problem that your potential customers have, then you might not have a viable business idea.

To ensure that you are solving a real problem for your potential customers, a great step in the business planning process is to get away from your computer and actually go out and talk to potential customers. Validate the assumption that they have the problem. Sample their opinions on your proposed solution to check if you're on the right track. There may be need to adjust your plans at this point.

Then take the next step and present your potential solution to their problem. Is it a good fit for them? Is it easier to access than the current solution? Do they think it is cheaper and faster?

Once you have described your target market's problem, the next section of your business plan should describe your solution. Your solution is the product or service that you plan on offering to your customers. What is it and how is it offered? How exactly does it solve the problem that your customers have?

For some products and services, you might want to describe real cases or tell a story about a real user who will benefit from (and be willing to pay for) your solution.

For example:

"Mary Jane is a 35 year old married woman without a child after 3 years of marriage. She usually visits social media pages that offer advice on pregnancy and assisted reproductive technology. I am confident that she will patronize our free health information blog and eventually signup for our In-vitro-fertilization service because of its near-free costing".

Target market

Now that you have detailed your problem and solution in your business plan, the next thing your reader wants to see is the target market: Who are you selling to?

Depending on the type of business you are starting and the type of plan you are writing, you may not need to go into too much detail here. No matter what, you need to know who your customer is and have a rough estimate of how many of them there are. If there aren't enough customers for your product or service, that could be a warning sign.

Too small a market, you may not have a financial backer. Too bogus and ambiguous, your reader may not believe you. So, be careful and be real here.

Market analysis and market research

If you are going to do a market analysis, start with some research. First, identify your market segments and determine how big each segment is. A market segment is a group of people (or other businesses) that you could potentially sell to.

Don't fall into the trap of defining the market as "everyone." A classic example is a restaurant company. While it would be tempting for a restaurant to say that their target market is everyone who has a mouth and a stomach, realistically they need to target a specific segment of the market in order to be successful.

Perhaps they need to target first-class citizens who want fine dining services; or busy business people and workers who need lunch during work breaks; or perhaps they are targeting Chinese with continental dishes.

Learn more about target marketing in this article.

TAM, SAM, and SOM

A good business plan will identify the target market segments and then provide some data to indicate how fast each segment is growing. When identifying target markets, a classic method is to use the TAM, SAM, and SOM breakdown to look at market sizes from a top-down approach as well as a bottom-up approach.

Here are some quick definitions:

TAM: Your Total Available or Addressable Market (everyone you wish to reach with your product)

SAM: Your Segmented Addressable Market or Served Available Market (the portion of TAM you will target)

SOM: Your Share Of the Market (the subset of your SAM that you will realistically reach - particularly in the first few years of your business).

For an existing business, the SOM is your actual share of the market.

Your ideal customer

When you have your target market segments defined, you need to define your ideal customer for each segment. At this point, you should discuss the trends for these markets. Are they growing or shrinking? Talk about the market's evolving needs, tastes, or other upcoming changes to the market.

One way to talk about your ideal customer in your plan is to use your "buyer persona" or "user persona." A buyer persona is a fictitious representation of your potential customers - they get a name, gender, income level, likes, dislikes, and so on.

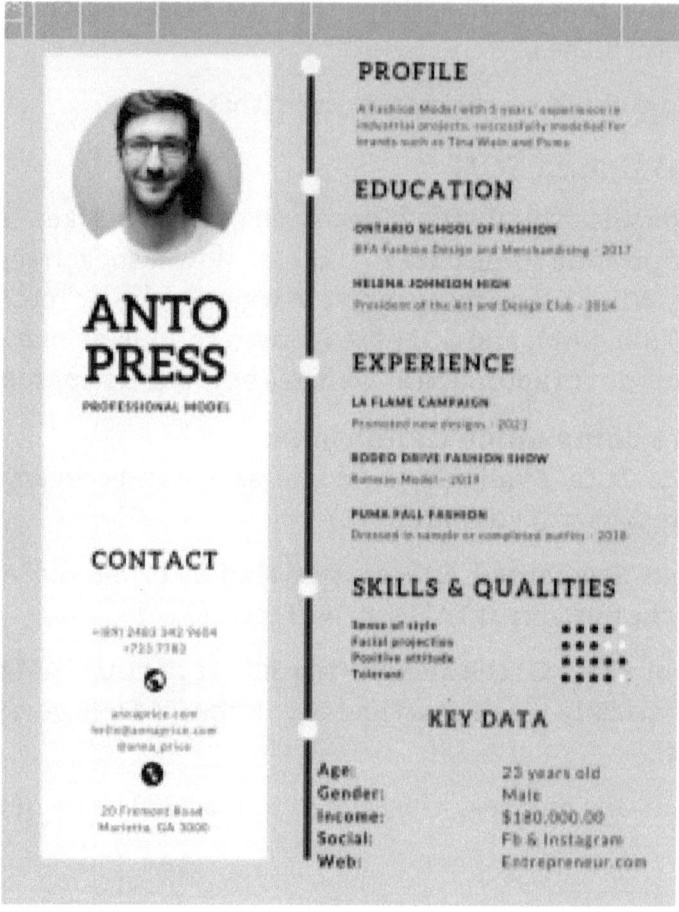

Buyer Persona

Pro Tip:

While this may seem like additional work on top of the market segmentation that you have already done, having a solid buyer persona will be an extremely useful tool to help you identify the marketing and sales tactics you'll need to use to attract these ideal customers. And the person reading your business plan will rate you highly for it.

Key customers

The final section of your target market segment should discuss key customers.

This section is really only required for enterprise (large) companies that have very few customers. Most small businesses and typical startups can skip this and move on.

But if you are selling to other businesses (B2B), you may have a few key customers that are critical to the success of your business, or a handful of important customers that are trend leaders in your space. If so, use this final portion of your target market segment to provide details about those customers and how they are important to your business's success.

Competition

You should describe your competition immediately your target market section has been defined. Who else is providing solutions to try and solve your customers' pain points? What are your competitive advantages over the competition?

The most important thing to show in this section of your business plan is how your solution is different or better than others that a potential customer might consider. Investors will want to know what advantages you have over the competition and how you plan on differentiating yourself.

One of the biggest mistakes entrepreneurs make in their business plans is stating that they don't have any competition.

The simple fact is that all businesses have competition. Competitors may not always come in the form of "direct competition," which is when you have a competitor offering a similar solution to your offering. Often times, you may be dealing with "indirect competition," which is when consumers solve their problem with an entirely different kind of solution.

For example, when AT&T was first marketing their mobile phones in the 1940's, there was no direct competition from other mobile phone manufacturers – there weren't any other mobile phones. Instead, AT&T was competing against other modes of distant communication – letter writing, table-top telephones and fax.

On the surface, none of these means of communication looked like real direct competition, but they were how people were solving their communication problems at the time. Thus, some people will choose the other means over AT&T mobile phones either because of the cost, ease/familiarity of use, or even superstition!

Future products and services

All entrepreneurs have a vision of where they want to take the business in the future if they are successful.

While it's tempting to spend a lot of time exploring future opportunities for new products and services, you shouldn't expand too much on these ideas in your business plan. It's certainly useful to include a paragraph or two about potential future plans, to show investors where you are headed in the long term, but you don't want your plan to be dominated by long-range plans that may or may not come to fruition. The focus should be on bringing your first products and services to market.

That is why the next section of your business plan is very crucial. Let us move on then...

CHAPTER FOUR
Execution

This chapter should contain comprehensive details about how you're actually going to make your business work. You'll cover your marketing and sales plans, operations, how you'll measure success, and the key milestones that you expect to achieve.

Marketing and sales plan

Outline details on how you plan to reach your target market segments (also called target marketing), how you plan on selling to those target markets, what your pricing plan is, and what types of activities and partnerships you need to make your business a success. This is the whole essence of defining your target market very well and having your buyer persona(s) fleshed out.

Your positioning statement

The first part of your marketing and sales plan is your positioning statement. Positioning is how you will try and present your company to your customers. Are you the low-price solution, or are you the premium, luxury brand in your market? Do you offer something that your competitors don't offer?

Before you start working on your positioning statement, you should take a little time to evaluate the current market and answer the following questions:

1. What features or benefits do you offer that your competitors do not?
2. What are your customers' primary needs and wants?
3. How are your competitors positioning themselves?
4. How do you plan on differentiating from the competition? In other words, why should a customer choose you instead of someone else?
5. Where do you see your company in the landscape of other solutions?

Once you've answered these questions, you can then work on your positioning strategy and define it in your business plan.

Don't worry about making your positioning statement very long or in-depth. You just need to explain where your company sits within the competitive landscape and what your core value proposition is that differentiates your company from the alternatives that a customer might consider.

You can use this simple formula to develop a positioning statement:

For (target market description) who (target market need), (this product) (how it meets the need). Unlike (key competition), it (most important distinguishing feature).

For example:

For (non-tech savvy small business owners) who (need a website and social media presence), (our digital marketing service) (will help them design a Wordpress website and create social media profiles). Unlike (other website designers and social media consultants), our service (includes training for clients' staff to enable them manage the platforms even after we have launched the projects).

Cool, right? Yeah.

Pricing

Once your reader knows what your overall positioning strategy is, they want to see your pricing structure.

Your positioning strategy will often be a major driver of the price you are offering. Price sends a very strong message to consumers and can be an important tool to communicate your positioning to consumers. If you are offering a premium product, a premium price will quickly communicate that message to consumers.

Deciding on your price can feel more like an art than a science, but there are some basic rules that you should follow:

1. Covering your costs
There are certain exceptions to this, but for the most part, you should be charging your customers more than it costs you to deliver your product or service.

2. Primary and secondary profit center pricing
Your initial price may not be your primary profit center. For example, you may sell your product at, or even below, your cost, but require a much more profitable maintenance or support contract to go along with the purchase.

For example, if you are a website developer, you may charge just what it cost you to register a domain name, host the website, and design the required pages without making much profit. Then you will offer monthly website maintenance services charged at a premium fee. You can even use your affiliate links to buy the domain name and web hosting services so that each time your client renews, you earn a commission.

3. Matching the market rate
Your prices need to match up with consumer demand and expectations. Price too high and you may have no customers. Price too low and people may undervalue your offering.

Let us briefly take a look at some best approaches to pricing.

3 approaches to pricing strategy

1. Cost-plus pricing
You can establish your pricing based on several factors. You can

look at your costs and then mark up your offering from there. This is usually called "cost-plus pricing" and can be effective for manufacturers where covering initial costs is critical.

2. Market-based pricing

Another method is to look at the current landscape of competitors and then price based on what the market is expecting. You could price at the high-end or low-end of the market to establish your positioning.

3. Value pricing

Yet another method is to look at a "value pricing" model where you determine the price base on how much value you are providing to your customer. For example, if you are marketing babysitting to working mums, you may be saving your clients 8 hour/week. If an hour of their time is valued at $20/hour, your service could charge $10/hour.

Clearly state your pricing structure and why you are going that route.

In addition, if you are going to have a tiered-pricing system, you should explain why and how it will work.

Promotion

With pricing and positioning taken care of, it's time to look at your promotion strategy. A promotion plan details how you plan on communicating with your prospects and customers. Remember, it's important that you measure how much your promotions cost and how many sales they deliver.

Here are a few areas that you might consider as part of your promotional plan:

Packaging

If you are selling a product, the packaging of that product is critical. If you have images of your packaging, including those in your business plan is always a good idea.

Be sure the packaging section of your plan answers the following questions:

1. Does your packaging match your positioning strategy?
2. How does your packaging communicate your key value proposition?
3. How does your packaging compare to your competition?

Advertising
Your business plan should include an overview of the kinds of advertising you plan to spend money on. Will you be advertising online? Or perhaps in traditional, offline media?

Public relations
Getting the media to cover you – PR - can be a great way to reach your customers. Getting a prominent review of your product or

service can give you the exposure you need to grow your business. If public relation is part of your promotional strategy, detail your plans here.

Content marketing

A popular strategy for promotion is engaging in what is called content marketing.

Content marketing is when you publish useful information, tips, and advice - usually made available for free - so that your target market can get to know your company through the expertise that you deliver. Content marketing is about teaching and educating your prospects on topics that they are interested in, not just on the features and benefits that you offer.

When you have them hooked with such content, you can then offer them your products/services.

Social media marketing

These days, having a social media presence is essentially a requirement for the vast majority of businesses.

You don't need to be on every social media channel, but you do need to be on the ones that your customers are active on. More and more prospects are using social media to learn about companies and to find out how responsive they are.

Craft a good social media strategy and explain it here. If you need help with doing this, contact me and I will help you with it.

Strategic alliances

As part of your marketing plan, you may rely on working closely with another company in a form of partnership.

This partnership may help provide access to a target market segment for your company while allowing your partner to offer a new product or service to their customers.

If you have partnerships already established, it's important to detail those partnerships in your business plan. If you have plans to leverage such partnerships in the near future, let your reader know now.

Operations

The operations section is how your business works. It's the logistics, technology, and other nuts and bolts. Depending on the type of business you are starting, you may or may not need the following sections. Only include what you need and remove everything else.

Sourcing and fulfillment

If your company is buying the products it is selling from other vendors, it's important to include details on where your products are coming from, how they get delivered to you, and ultimately how you deliver the products to the customer - that's sourcing and fulfillment.

If you are sourcing products from manufacturers overseas, investors are going to want to know about your progress working with these suppliers. If your business is going to be delivering products to your customers, you should describe your plans for shipping your products.

Pro tip:

This section is a must-have if you are an ecommerce store buying products from China or anywhere else abroad.

Technology

If you are a technology company, it's critical for your business plan to describe your technology and what your "secret formula" is.

Don't give away trade secrets in your business plan, but try to describe how your technology is different and better than other solutions out there. Endeavor to describe how your technology works.

Pro tip:

You don't need to go into excruciating detail here though, if an investor is interested in more detail they will ask for it, that way you can protect your intellectual property.

Distribution

For product companies, a distribution plan is an important part of the complete business plan. For the most part, service companies can skip this piece and move on.

Distribution is how you will get your product into the hands of your customers. Every industry has different distribution channels and the best way to create your distribution plan is to interview others in your industry to figure out what their distribution model is.

Here are a few common distribution models that you may consider for your business:

Direct distribution
Selling directly to consumers is by far the most simple and most profitable option. Is this the model you are adopting? Let your reader know.

Retail distribution
Most large retailers don't like the hassle of dealing with thousands of individual suppliers.

Instead, they prefer to buy through large distribution companies that aggregate products from lots of suppliers and then make that inventory available to retailers to purchase. Of course, these distributors take a percentage of the sales that pass through their warehouses.

Manufacturers' representatives
These are typically salespeople who work as sales reps. They often have relationships with retailers and distributors and work

to sell your products into the appropriate channel. They typically work on commission and it's not uncommon for a representative to be necessary for getting a new company access to a distributor or retailer.

OEM

This stands for "Original Equipment Manufacturer." If your product is sold to another company that then incorporates your product into their finished product, then you are using an OEM channel.

A good example of this is Smartphone Integrated Circuits manufacturers. While big phone companies like Samsung and Techno build large components of their phones, they also purchase ICs from third-party vendors and incorporate those parts into the finished phone.

Note:

Most companies use a mixture of distribution channels as part of their plans, so don't feel that you need to be limited to a single channel. For example, it is very common to both sell direct and via distributors. For instance, you can purchase a Toyota car directly from Toyota, or go into an Elizade car stand and get one

Milestones and metrics

Without a reasonable schedule, defined roles, key responsibilities and some clear path to get the work done, a business plan is only a document on paper.

While the milestones and metrics section of your business plan may not be long, it's critical that you take the time to look forward and schedule the next critical steps for your business. Your reader will want to see that you understand what needs to happen to make your plans a reality and that you are working on a realistic schedule.

Start with a quick review of your milestones. Milestones are planned major goals. For example, if you are producing a vaccine for Covid-19, you will have milestones associated with clinical testing, CDC approvals and government approval processes. If you are creating an online course, you may have milestones associated with researching your students' needs, writing your lecture notes, and recording your lectures on video.

Traction

While milestones look forward, you will also want to take a look back at major accomplishments that you have already had. This is usually known as "traction." What evidence of success have your business had?

Note:

Traction could be some initial sales, a successful test of a product, or a significant partnership. Sharing this proof that your company is more than just an idea - that it has actual evidence that it is going to be a success - can be critically important to landing the money you need to grow your business.

Key performance indicators (KPIs)

In addition to milestones and traction, your business plan should detail the key performance indicators that you will be monitoring as your business takes off. These metrics are the numbers that you monitor on a regular basis to judge the health of your business. They are the drivers of growth for your business model and your financial plan.

For example, an ecommerce store may pay special attention to the number of visitors to their online store to the ratio of sales. We call this conversion optimization in online business terms.

Pro Tip:

The main KPIs in your business may be different to the ones another business may measure. So, take your time and think this through. Don't just copy and paste something you see on Google, this is a sure way to have your business plan trashed!

Key assumptions and risks

Finally, your business plan should detail the key assumptions you have made that are important for your businesses success.

Knowing what your assumptions are as you start a business can make the difference between business success and business failure. When you recognize your assumptions, you can set out to prove that your assumptions are correct.

Pro Tip:

Think about key assumptions as risks. What risks are you taking with your business? For example, if you don't have a proven demand for a new product, you are making an assumption that people will want what you are building.

If you are relying on content marketing as a major promotional channel, you are making assumptions that SEO and paid ads will always be effective and that website visitors will actually make a purchase.

CHAPTER FIVE
Company Overview and Team

In this chapter, you'll review the structure of your company and who the key team members are. These details are especially important to investors and bankers as they'll want to know who's behind the company and if they can convert a good idea into a great business.

Team

There is this old adage that investors don't invest in ideas, they invest in people. Some investors even go as far as to say that they would rather invest in a mediocre idea with a great team behind it than a blockbuster idea with a mediocre team.

What this really means is that running a successful business all comes down to getting the work done. Can you actually accomplish what you have planned? Do you have the right team in place to turn a good idea into a great business that will have customers queuing in front of your doors?

The company overview and team chapter of your business plan is where you make your best case that you have the right team in place to execute on your idea. It should show that you have thought about the important roles and responsibilities your business needs in order to grow and be successful.

Include brief bios that highlight relevant experiences of each key team member. It's important here to make the case for why the team is the right team to turn an idea into a reality. Do they have the right industry experience and background? Have members of the team had entrepreneurial successes before? Have they demonstrated leadership and ability in other areas of their career?

Pro Tip:

A common mistake novice entrepreneurs make in describing the management team is giving everyone on the team a C-level title (CEO, CMO, COO, and so on). While this might be good for egos, it's often not realistic. And it may make you appear mediocre in front of potential investors.

As a company grows, you may require different types of experience and knowledge. It's often better to allow for future growth of titles rather than to start everyone at the top with no room for future growth or change.

Note:

Your management team doesn't necessarily need to be complete in order to have a complete business plan. If you know that you have a management team gap that needs filling it is still okay. In fact, investors see the fact that you know you are missing certain key people as a sign of maturity and knowledge about what your business needs to succeed. If you do have gaps in your team, simply identify them and indicate that you are looking for the right people to fill certain roles.

Finally, you may choose to include a proposed organizational chart in your business plan. This isn't critical and can certainly be placed in your business plan's appendix. In any case, at some point, as you explore funding options, you may be asked for an "organizational chart," so it's good to have one ready.

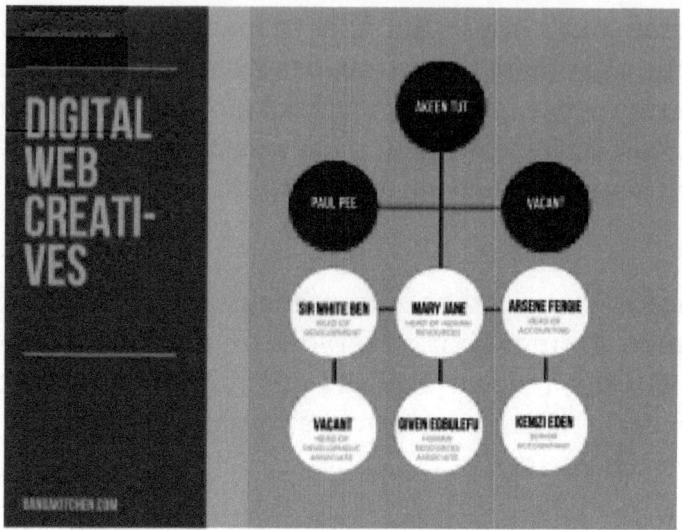

Organizational Chart

Pro Tip:

Beyond raising money, an organizational chart is also a useful planning tool to help you think about your company and how it will grow over time. What key roles will you be looking to fill in the future and how will you structure your teams to get the most out of them? An organizational chart can help you think through these questions.

Company overview

The company overview will most likely be the shortest section of your business plan. For a plan that you intend to just share internally with your business partners and team members, skip this section and move on.

For a plan that you will share with people outside of your company, this section should include:

1. Mission statement
2. Intellectual property

3. A review of your company's legal structure and ownership
4. The business location
5. A brief history of the company if it's an existing company

Mission statement

Don't fall into the trap of spending a day or more on your mission statement. An hour or two should be plenty of time.

Avoid putting together a long, generic statement about how your company is serving its customers, employees, and so on. Your company mission should be short - one or two sentences at most - and it should encompass, at a very high level, what you are trying to do. Frankly, your mission statement and your overall value proposition might even be the same thing.

Here at StartUP Crest, our mission statement is this: "Help young people and small business owners' transition from frustrated start-ups to successful entrepreneurs." It's simple and encompasses everything we do from the types of products that we build to the kind of marketing that we do.

Intellectual property

This mostly applies to technology and scientific ventures, so just skip this if you don't need to discuss your patents and other intellectual property.

But, if you have intellectual property that is proprietary to your business and helps your business defend it against competitors; you should detail that information here. If you have patents or pending patents, this is the place to highlight those patents.

Equally important to discuss is technology licensing - if you are licensing core technology from someone else, you need to disclose that in your business plan and be sure to include details of the partnership.

Business structure and ownership

Your company overview should also include a summary of your company's current business structure. Are you a Limited Liability Company? A Corporation? An Enterprise? A Sole Proprietorship? In a Partnership? State it here.

Be sure to provide a review of how the business is owned as well. Does each business partner own an equal portion of the business? How is ownership divided? Potential lenders and investors will want to know the structure of the business before they will consider a loan or investment.

Company history

If you are writing a business plan for an existing company, it's appropriate to include a brief history of the company and highlight major historical achievements. Again, keep this section short - no more than a few paragraph at most.

This section is especially useful to give context to the rest of your plan, and can also be very useful for internal plans. The company history section can provide new employees with a background on the company so that they have a better context for the work that they are doing and where the company has come from over the years.

Location

Finally, the company overview section of your business plan should describe your current location and any facilities that the company owns.

For businesses that serve consumers from a storefront, this information is critical. Also, for businesses that require large facilities for manufacturing, warehousing, and so on, this information is an important part of your plan. Skip it and you appear not serious.

CHAPTER SIX
Financial plan

L ast, but certainly not least of 'the big four', is your financial plan chapter. This is often what entrepreneurs find most daunting, but it doesn't have to be as intimidating as it seems. Business financials for most startups are less complicated than you think, and a business degree is certainly not required to build a solid financial forecast.

That said, if you need additional help, there are plenty of tools and resources out there to help you build a solid financial plan.

A typical financial plan will have monthly sales and revenue projections for the first 12 months, and then annual projections for the remaining three to five years. Three-year projections are typically adequate, but some investors will request a five-year forecast.

Following are details of the financial statements that you should include in your business plan, and a brief overview of what should be in each section.

Sales forecast

Your sales forecast is just that - your projections of how much you are going to sell over the next few years.

A sales forecast is typically broken down into several rows, with a row for each core product or service that you are offering. Don't make the mistake of breaking down your sales forecast into excruciating detail. Just focus on the high-level at this point.

For example, if you are forecasting sales for a restaurant, you might break down your forecast into these groups: lunch, dinner, and drinks. If you are a product company, you could break down your forecast by target market segments or into major product categories.

Your sales forecast will also include a corresponding row for each sales row to cover Cost of Goods Sold, also known as COGS (also called direct costs). These rows show the expenses related to making your product or delivering your service. COGS should only include those costs directly related to making your products, not regular business expenses such as rent, insurance, salaries, etc.

For a restaurant, it would be the cost of groceries and food ingredients. For a product company, it would include the cost of raw materials. For a consulting business, it might be the cost of paper and other presentation materials.

Sales Forecast

Personnel plan

Your personnel plan details how much you plan on paying your employees. For a small company, you might list every position on the personnel plan and how much will be paid each month for each position. For a larger company, the personnel plan is typically broken down into functional groups such as "admin", "marketing" and "sales."

The personnel plan will also include what is typically called "employee burden," which is the cost of an employee beyond salary. This includes payroll taxes, insurance, and other necessary costs that you will incur every month for having an employee on your payroll.

Payroll Years 1-3

Prepared By:
Mary Jane

Company Name:
Health Hub

Employee Types	Year 1 Totals	Growth Rate 1 to 2	Second Year	Rate 2 to 3	Third Year
Owner(s)	5,200	30.0%	6,760	50.0%	10,140
Full-Time Employees	93,600	10.0%	102,960	20.0%	123,552
Part-Time Employees	7,800	10.0%	8,580	20.0%	10,296
Independent Contractors	3,120	5.0%	3,276	5.0%	3,440
Total Salaries and Wages	$ 109,720		$ 121,576		$ 147,428
Payroll Taxes and Benefits					
Social Security	6,609	20.0%	7,931	30.0%	10,310
Medicare	-	20.0%	-	30.0%	-
Federal Unemployment Tax (FUTA)	462	20.0%	554	30.0%	721
State Unemployment Tax (SUTA)	2,657	20.0%	3,188	30.0%	4,144
Employee Pension Programs	8,528	0.0%	8,528	0.0%	8,528
Worker's Compensation	5,330	3.0%	5,490	3.0%	5,655
Employee Health Insurance	5,330	3.0%	5,490	3.0%	5,655
Other Employee Benefit Programs	-	0.0%	-	0.0%	-
Total Payroll Taxes and Benefits	$ 28,916		$ 31,181		$ 35,012
Total Salaries and Related Expenses	$ 138,636		$ 152,757		$ 182,440

Personnel Plan

Profit and loss statement

Also known as the income statement, the profit and loss (or P&L) is where your numbers all come together and show if you're making a profit or taking a loss. The P&L pulls data from your sales forecast and your personnel plan and also includes a list of all your other ongoing expenses associated with running your business.

The P&L also contains the all-important "bottom line" where your expenses are subtracted from your earnings to show if your business is making a profit each month or potentially incurring some losses while you grow.

A typical P&L will be a spreadsheet that includes the following:

1. Sales (or income or revenue). This number will come from your sales forecast worksheet and includes all revenue generated by the business.

2. Cost of goods sold (COGS). This number also comes from your sales forecast and it is the total cost of selling your product. For service businesses, this can also be called cost of sales or direct costs.

3. Gross margin. Subtract your COGS from your sales to get this number. Most profit and loss statements also show this number as a percentage of total sales (gross margin / sales = gross margin percent)

4. Operating expenses. List all of your expenses associated with running your business, excluding the COGS that you already detailed. You should also exclude taxes, depreciation, and amortization. However, you should include salaries, research and development (R&D) expenses, marketing expenses, and other expenses here.

5. Total operating expenses. This is the sum of your operating expenses.

6. Operating income. This is also known as EBITDA or earnings before interest, taxes, depreciation, and amortization. This is a simple calculation where you just subtract your total operating expenses and COGS from your sales.

7. Interest, taxes, depreciation, and amortization. If you have any of these expense streams, you will list them below your operating income.

8. Total expenses. Add your operating expenses to interest, taxes,

depreciation, and amortization to get your total expenses.

9. Net profit. This is the all-important bottom line that shows if you've made a profit, or taken a loss, during a given month or year.

P&L

◆ ◆ ◆

Cash flow statement

The cash flow statement often gets confused with the profit and loss statement, but they are very different and serve very different purposes. While the P&L calculates your profits and losses, the cash flow statement keeps track of how much cash (money in the bank) that you have at any given point.

The key to understanding the difference between the two statements is understanding the difference between "cash" and "profits". The simplest way to think about it is when you make a sale. If you need to send a bill to your customer and then your customer takes 30 or 60 days to pay the bill, you don't have the cash from the sale right away. But, you will have booked the sale in your P&L and shown a profit from that sale the day you made the sale.

A typical cash flow statement starts with the amount of cash you have on hand, adds new cash received through cash sales and paid invoices, and then subtracts cash that you have paid out as you pay bills, pay off loans, pay taxes, etc. This will then leave you with your total cash flow (cash in minus cash out) and your ending cash which is, starting cash + cash in – cash out = ending cash).

Your cash flow statement will show you when you might be low on cash, and when it might be the best time to buy new equipment. Above all, your cash flow statement will help you figure out how much money you might need to raise or borrow to grow your company.

Since an operating business can't run out of cash without having to close its doors, use your cash flow statement to figure out your low cash points and consider options to bring in additional cash.

Cashflow Statement

Balance sheet

The last financial statement that most businesses will need to create as part of their business plan is the balance sheet. The balance sheet provides an overview of the financial health of your business. It lists the assets in your company, the liabilities, and your (the owner's) equity. If you subtract the company's liabilities from assets, you can determine the net worth of the company.

Instead of providing additional detail on the balance sheet here, I'll refer you to this article on building and reading balance sheets.

Balance Sheet Years 1-3

Prepared By:
Mary Jane

Company Name:
Health Hub

ASSETS	2020	2021	2022
Current Assets			
Cash	18,067	21,481	17,250
Accounts Receivable	-	-	-
Inventory	-	-	-
Prepaid Expenses	533	267	-
Other Initial Costs	333	167	-
Total Current Assets $	18,933 $	21,914 $	17,250
Fixed Assets			
Real Estate – Land	-	-	-
Real Estate – Buildings	-	-	-
Leasehold Improvements	-	-	-
Equipment	2,600	4,600	7,600
Furniture and Fixtures	3,000	4,000	5,000
Vehicles	5,000	10,000	15,000
Other	1,500	1,500	1,500
Total Fixed Assets $	12,100 $	20,100 $	29,100
(Less Accumulated Depreciation) $	1,033 $	4,110 $	8,749
Total Assets $	29,999 $	37,904 $	37,601
LIABILITIES & EQUITY			
Liabilities			
Accounts Payable	-	-	-
Commercial Loan Balance	-	-	-
Commercial Mortgage Balance	-	-	-
Credit Card Debt Balance	-	-	-
Vehicle Loan Balance	-	-	-
Other Bank Debt Balance	-	-	-
Line of Credit Balance	48,806	97,234	160,997
Total Liabilities $	48,806 $	97,234 $	160,997
Equity			
Common Stock	12,800	12,800	12,800
Retained Earnings	(31,606)	(72,129)	(136,196)
Dividends Dispersed/Owners Draw			
Total Equity $	(18,806) $	(59,329) $	(123,396)
Total Liabilities and Equity $	29,999 $	37,904 $	37,601
	$ - $	- $	- $
Balance sheet in or out of balance?	Balanced!	Balanced!	Balanced!

Balance Sheet

Use of funds

If the purpose of your business plan is raising money from investors, you should include a brief section in your business plan that details exactly how you plan on using your investors' cash.

This section doesn't need to go into excruciating detail about how every last dollar will be spent, but instead, show the major areas where the investors' funds will be spent. These could include marketing, R&D, sales, or perhaps purchasing inventory.

Exit strategy

The last thing that you might need to include in your financial plan chapter is a section on your exit strategy.

An exit strategy is your plan for eventually selling your business, either to another company or to the public in an IPO. If you have investors, they will want to know your thoughts on this. If you're running a business that you plan to maintain ownership of indefinitely, and you're not seeking angel investment or VC funding, you can skip the exit strategy section.

However, if you need outside investment, it is a must. After all, your investors will want to get a return on their investment, and the only way they will get this is if the company is sold to someone else.

Again, you don't need to go into excruciating detail here, but you should identify some companies that might be interested in buying you if you are successful.

CHAPTER SEVEN
Appendix

An appendix to your business plan isn't a required chapter by any means, but it is a useful place to stick any charts, tables, definitions, legal notes, or other critical information that either felt too long or too out-of-place to include elsewhere in your business plan. If you have a patent or a patent pending, or illustrations of your product, this is where you'd want to include the details.

Further reading

If you want even more details on creating your business plan, please take a look at these articles. They will guide you through the details of creating a winning plan that will impress your investors:

1. Calculating breakeven point

2. The Business Model Canvas

3. How to Pitch to Investors – Public Speaking

4. Options for Funding Your Business

5. Business Plan Dos and Don'ts

PART THREE: ADDITIONAL GUIDELINES

I n this third and final section, I will provide you with some more guidelines to help you finish your business plan.

CHAPTER EIGHT
Common Business Plan Mistakes and How to Avoid Them

If you have ever written a business plan that was rejected, you probably made one or more of these business plan mistakes. They are common but can be easily avoided if you know what to do.

So, in this chapter I am going to share with you 11 common business plan mistakes and how you can avoid them. This chapter is part of my Business Planning Guide, where you find everything you need to know about planning your business.

1. Slacky Executive Summary

In many business plans, the executive summary is poorly written; lacking key ingredients that will hook the reader.

The executive summary is where you introduce yourself and your business to the reader. Make sure you are creating the best "first impressions". Bankers, Investors and other top executives that will read your plan are very busy people, if you fail to impress them here, they will dump the document and not bother with the other parts.

So, make your executive summary punchy, succinct and interest-arousing!

Pro Tip:

Ask a professional business plan developer to take a look at this section for you. They may ask for a small fee, but it will be worth it in the end.

2. Vague Definition of Target Market

Every business is supposed to solve a need/problem for a particular market. The problem and the market must be clearly identified in your business plan. Do not make the mistake of saying that everyone needs your service.

Even if you are selling oxygen that people breathe in for life, not everyone wants to buy your oxygen. Some people will prefer to die than buy from you. The reader will want to see specifically who needs your service and if you can reach them with your marketing and distribution channels.

3. Unrealistic Business Growth Forecast

This is a very common mistake. Because you want to make your business and your team look very good you will forecast growth that even established businesses in your industry cannot dream of.

The people reading your business plan will almost always understand the industry more than you do. You will be wasting your time trying to convince them that your business will out-perform every index in the market.

Pro Tip:

If you strongly believe that your business will perform the way you are projecting, put it there. But you had better have data to back it up!

4. Lack of Data-Driven Assumptions

Every assumption you make in your business plan must be backed with data. The data could be from your business history or from industry reports.

Bankers and investors love business plans that have the required data to support their assumptions. This alone can stand you out from the crowd.

5. Playing Down Risks and Over-blowing Opportunities

This is very common with business plans seeking loans and investments. You will read statements like,

"Even if the government increases tariffs on importation of spare parts we will continue to be profitable because we can always increase our prices"!

Seriously, and you don't think that an increase in price will push the customers to buy the next best alternative? Well, your reader will not agree with you; even if you are the sole distributor of that product. There will always be alternatives that the customer can use.

6. Writing off the Competition

Every business has competition. Even if you are the only Patent Medicine Store in a small town, the people have the option of patronizing herbal treatments by herbalists.

It is true that competition is stiffer in some markets than others. But never make the mistake of dismissing the competition.

Pro Tip:

Statements like "competition is very low", "the existing companies have inferior products", and "we are the sole distributors of this product" tend to sound dismissive of the competition.

Ditch them for phrases like "even though we have the best quality product, we realize that the competition..." or "While there are not so many players in the market, new entrants may still pose competition threat".

You get the idea? Acknowledge the competition while highlighting your opportunity.

7. Too much Detail on Product/Service Description

Some startups are so fascinated about their product and ideas that they go on and on singing about their features in the business plan. And to make matters worse, they gloss over the systems and operations required to deliver the product to the target market.

This is a very big mistake when writing a business plan. The reader will want to know about the product, but they will be more interested in how you will deliver it to the market and make money from it. So, focus more on the systems and operations, but less on the product/idea.

Pro Tip:

Use the appendix section to add any more details about your product. If the reader likes your business plan, they will dig deeper in this section.

8. Using a Generic Business Plan Template

Many people download a business plan template from the internet; fill up some stuff and boom! They have a business plan ready. No, my friend.

You see, a business plan is written for a particular purpose. The template you just downloaded may not be fine-tuned towards your purpose of writing a business plan. For example, business plans that are written to secure a bank loan will be conservative and risks averse, whereas those written to secure equity investments tend to highlight opportunities creatively and realistically.

Thus, using a generic template can make you miss out in highlighting what is more important.

9. Too Much Focus on Profitability as Against Cashflow

It is true that the bottom-line of being in business is to be profitable. So, your business plan must show how you will turn a profit. However, focusing too much on profitability can force you to make over-ambitious assumptions and projections.

Instead of focusing on profits, focus on regular and consistent cash flow. So long as your business plan shows that your business will always have cash to operate seamlessly, many bankers and investors will like it.

10. Ambiguous goals and Objectives

Like unrealistic projections, many business plans also have goals and objectives that are bogus with lots of ambiguity.

Make sure all your goals are S.M.A.R.T.

S.M.A.R.T. being acronym for:

S - Specific

M - Measurable

A - Attainable

R - Realistic

T - Time-bound

11. Poorly Written and Formatted

An investor or a banker will quickly trash your business plan if you cannot construct simple sentences. It will be even worse if you format the document poorly by referencing wrong or non-existent page numbers and pictures.

Please, take the time to read your plan carefully. If possible, have another pair of eyes to proofread your grammar and spellings.

Pro Tip:

You can use a tool like grammarly to also proofread your writings.

ABOUT THE AUTHOR

| Entrepreneur | Public Speaker |Business Coach

Eduzobe Jahswill Udogbo (StartUP Jahswill) is a trained Physicist with a passion for building and growing small businesses.

He is the CEO of StartUP Crest, a company he formed to help young people start and grow small businesses.

He is also the CEO of LabHub Medical Laboratories and Diagnostics and the founding Managing Partner/General Manager of Karone Photo World Ltd, both very successful startups.

In 2009 he setup his first registered company, SwiftTech Integrated Solutions Ltd with the aim of providing alternative power supply to residents of the satellite towns around the Nigerian capital territory, Abuja.

Although that venture turned out to be a total failure, Jahswill learned valuable lessons that have helped him to start and grow other businesses with varied degrees of success.

His number one desire is to help as many young people as possible to discover their entrepreneurial skills and use this to start and grow businesses that will provide employment and livelihood.

His mission is simple: help young people transition from frustrated job seekers and disillusioned startups to successful entrepreneurs.

He promotes financial education that helps young people understand the career options available to them as a means of creating wealth as opposed to the old one-way thinking of "Go to School, get a good job and live comfortably ever after"! Jahswill appreciates that while university/college education might be a necessity in some chosen careers, it is just one of the options and not the surest path to creating wealth. That is why he advocates learning business and financial skills that gives the best and surest path to wealth creation.

He spends most of his time developing content for his various educational platforms especially his blog www.startup-crest.com where he provides valuable resources for startups.

He is happily married and blessed with a beautiful daughter.